The Fifth House Tilts

The Fifth House Tilts

Poems by

Peggy Hammond

© 2022 Peggy Hammond. All rights reserved.
This material may not be reproduced in any form, published,
reprinted, recorded, performed, broadcast,
rewritten or redistributed without
the explicit permission of Peggy Hammond.
All such actions are strictly prohibited by law.

Cover design by Shay Culligan
Cover art by Tim Mossholder
Author's photo by Chelsea Lane

ISBN: 978-1-63980-145-9

Kelsay Books
502 South 1040 East, A-119
American Fork, Utah 84003
Kelsaybooks.com

Acknowledgments

This collection would not exist had I not been inspired by the life of Sylvia Plath; her art continues to be admired by so many. To my husband, thank you for always cheering me forward.

Heartfelt thanks to the editors of the following journals for first publication of these poems, some in different versions:

Rogue Agent: "Surfaces" (Prologue)

Ginosko Literary Journal: "At the end," "Transformation"

Trouvaille Review: "Flirtation"

Amethyst Review: "The Nature of Things"

The Comstock Review: "Warrior"

River City Poetry: "Testify," "Moment of Stillness," "Sunset Blessing"

Adelaide Literary Magazine: "Husk," "Tsunami," "Three Days," "The Fall"

The Raven's Perch Literary Magazine: "Division"

Scissortail Quarterly: "Ebb," "Aphrodite"

Eunoia Review: "Surrender"

For Women Who Roar: "Green Drake"

Contents

Prologue: Surfaces, i   13

Marking Territory

Resurrection   17
Flirtation   18
Risk   20
Alhambra   21

Violations

Green Drake   25
Postmortem   26
Change   27
Husk   28
Dragonfly   29
Exit   31
Tsunami   32
Testify   33
Three Days   34

The Footings Give Way

Waiting   37
The Fall   38
Doubts   39
Force   40
Division   41
At the end   42
Uprooted   43

Inaccessible

Warrior	47
Moment of Stillness	49
Lullaby	50
Unmoored	51
Without	52
Surrender	53
Ebb	54

Easements

Aphrodite	59
Transformation	60
Reach	61
The Nature of Things	62
Sunset Blessing	63

Epilogue: Surfaces, ii	65

"affairs of the heart are in the fifth house"

Corrine Lane, *12 Astrological Houses—Astrology Lesson 4*

Prologue: Surfaces, i

A half-day from here
there's a field that knows
each letter of my name,
knows the sinews
that catch and stitch
my bones one to the next.
Neither of us
will forget the other.
Even here,
inside this dark sleep,
I bolt upright;
blind as a mole,
I bump and clatter
my way out
to answer the call,
to stand
in thick moonlight
dripping though
early morning air.
Beside me,
in a gooseflesh breeze,
a chimney stone-stacked
and leaning
brushes at lichens rooted
to her granite eyes.
We comfort one another,
each the lone survivor
of what once was home,
each unwilling to crumble.

Marking Territory

Resurrection

When you find me
I am hollow,
nothing more than seeds
rattling in a dry shell.

Your sharp instinct knows
I have looked for nurturing soil,
something to coax out of me
the wholeness of being,
to join stem to leaf,
leaf to flower.

When I see you,
I understand.
I reassemble,
dandelion
canceling the dispersal.

You speak my name.
I resurrect:
arteries and veins,
airways and lungs
remember themselves;
blood pulses
oxygen moves
life expands.

Flirtation

This black sky
scattered with bright stars,
ink-dark carpet glittering
with unstrung pearls,
says nothing
as moonlight, a maiden trailing
white silk,
touches Earth, glides easily
down apple orchard's narrow row.
Gnarled mothers
burdened with green fruit
now flushing golden
allow the brush of moonbeams
along twisted branches.
They know the touch
is temporary flirtation.

In night's soft silence,
I cannot speak my wish:
a life with you, spinning
words and visions,
standing on one another's shoulders
to better view the most exquisite
seconds of this world's parade,
detaching from onlookers
to walk with musicians, dancers,
the sequined ones whose gaze
is turned toward the horizon.

If we keep open
this current between us,
our brightness will
burn and blaze
across the heavens.

But should the moon
lure your eye,
our light will dim
to the feeble glow
of creation's first stars.

Risk

I stand on the bank, afraid;
mud anchors my feet,
urging me to safety.
This river, mercurial,
deep, is no friend;
I am too weak
to protect against
this murmurer,
this fast talker.

But you are a water-bearer
and I have sworn allegiance.
Your words skip like smooth stones
across the stream's skin,
calming each current.

You take my hand;
wet earth softens its grip.
I lift away.
Gently, we step down.
Ankle-deep and refreshing.
You are trustworthy and I follow,
waist-deep now; already I forget
the feel of myself
weighted on land.

You begin to swim.
I drown my fear
and follow.

Alhambra

A plane deposits us in Spain's belly;
a train rocks us southbound.
Arriving at our hotel midafternoon
we reach for the Nasrid Palace,
the Alhambra, instead of our suitcase.
She sits on her hill as she has for hundreds of years,
the Sierra Nevada stretched behind her like a cloak
proffered by a suitor she is resisting.
You say she is waiting for us.

Her gardens are heavy with pink and red roses
dancing under fairy-tale blue sky.
Orderly fountains toss sprays of water
as if greeting us, the first newlyweds.
A dignified pool anchors a pillared walkway;
archways intricately carved drip lacy designs,
a grandmother's bridal veil.

In the evening, we dine too early, obvious tourists;
the waiter brings us small glasses of sherry
as if we are locals and know tradition.
I wish to impress you with knowledge of Amontillado
but see you watching a dark beauty strolling across the square;
her eyes lock with yours.

Your noticing another is not new; words
soaked with sherry and sadness die on my lips.

At the palace today, a guide explained Arabic inscriptions
flowing along walls, curving around columns:
There is no victor but Allah.

The Nasrids, understanding expulsion,
knew the value of diplomacy.

Perspective is needed when others desire
that which you think of as yours.

Violations

Green Drake

Purist, you spawned poems
with a typewriter.
No clues
when you left,
no answers
embedded in words
you cast as easily
as a lone fly fisher,
stance relaxed in the sun,
cap tugged low
to lessen the squint.

I was the shy trout,
my rainbow sides teasing
you in lusty dreams,
your silver words fluttering,
drawing me closer.
A Green Drake
I could not resist striking.

Purist, you gave line
enough to secure.
Your hard retrieve
taught the curve of the hook
in soft flesh.

When you lifted me in
your hand, my mouth,
sore and open,
pulled but found

no air to breathe.

Postmortem

All this, I learned long after
you cried in our yard, telling
me another had won your heart,
as if that beating muscle
were no more than a child's prize
dangling in a carnival-game tent.

Your mother, thinking you royalty,
always wished you'd chosen another.
My tiara, clearly fake, smiled
gap-toothed at her, a poor
relation needing dentures.
My hemline too ragged,
my curtsy embarrassing.

When my body hosted your son,
I gasped for air, then sickened on it.
You complained to friends I was
unattractively large; skin
so sickeningly stretched
stilled your desire.

What I did not say,
once you bestowed this knowing
carelessly folded into a letter,
is that time does not idly pass;
all the while she sharpens her knife;
at every chance her blade
slices to the bone.

Change

The days are different now,
the air, cooler.

Purple phlox once tall and proud
droops into garden path;

blossoms release like tears.
Summer fades to autumn;

the dying has begun.
Sunshine, rays anemic, weakens.

Change has arrived inside too;
no clatter of keyboard, no

midnight love and talk.
I endure your departure.

Dark nights, long and sleepless,
push me into motion.

Restless, I haunt moonlit rooms;
forgotten slip of paper,

small detritus,
sighs her name.

Husk

A fool's finger
slipped our wheel from its cog

and clockwork smooth life
shouted to a stop.

Now, without you,
I harvest a son's tears,

rid pantry shelves
of small hopes gone sour.

Outside, cicadas chorus incessantly.
One by one, backs split

and they emerge,
tender and new.

Inside, my own husk
pinches and binds,

my own song
rises and merges.

Dragonfly

I tried to see you
through the eyes of our son,
the swaddled bundle you
could not connect to,
stay with, love.
Holding him against my heart
as if his weight
could stop my life's blood
from spilling, as if
rhythmic beats
could soothe distress,
I focused on your movements:
hastily gathered books,
a bag filled with belts and shoes,
the emptying of a closet,
a marriage.

I tried to feel what he must,
that your affection demands
things he cannot understand
or deliver.

He is a dragonfly,
soft-bodied, vulnerable,
new wings woven of lace and hope,
not yet dry, unable to support.
He sits and waits,
dark eyes aware of motion,
the potential for danger:
will you admire his beauty
or swallow him whole,

leaving torn wings
discarded, too-soon decayed?
His stillness reveals knowing:
the creator is capable
of destruction.

Exit

You fumble with
the key to our house.
It proves difficult to discard.

You curse as it bests you,
refusing to yield its space.
A virgin, knees tightly clamped.

You pry apart metal lips,
slide key into open air,
drop it into my waiting palm.

It lies deflowered, exposed.

I blanket it with my fingers,
shield its weeping eye
against your departure.

Tsunami

Wishing a moment alone,
the sea releases
its grip on the shore.
One at a time,
long fingers indulgent
with starfish rings
lift, let go, recede.

Fish, draped in oranges,
blues and yellows,
withdraw to
quiet corners.

They know.

Moody silence deafens my ears.
Unschooled dirt dweller, I stand
entranced by sand uncovered,
indecent, blushing its remorse

while kelp ladies jostle,
lean into the pull,
green hair streaming,
toes curling for purchase.

When the sea rushes forward,
I break for air, watch as
you secure your own
current, and listen
for love
in the sea's jealous roar.

Testify

The funeral today
was not yours
but for a moment,
I imagine it might be.
If it were,
I would be the honored widow
embraced by others,
admired for bravery,
instead of what I am:
a woman wiping away traces
of a discarded marriage,
sticky and unyielding,
like sap from a pine.

Graveside,
we recite Psalm 23.
Images of valleys and shadows
pair perfectly with this day;
without effort, our voices
succumb to the cadence.

A highway spoons the cemetery;
the sound of wheels on asphalt
creates a refrain
but repeats too frequently,
unwelcome, loud.
Our lips move
but we are no longer heard.

The air beside me
testifies you are gone.

Three Days

An oak we planted
leans precariously
into areas not its own.

An expert arrives,
advises removal.
Clinical, he ticks off the steps.
Limbs shorn, trunk
cut into sections, hauled down.
And if I desire, the stump taken,
leaving a depression
which time will mend.

We decide. Three days from now.

That night
I observe the oak,
knowing it absorbed our plan
the way roots
take in groundwater.

Even now
its leaves droop,
its demise a certainty,
no power of its own.

The Footings Give Way

Waiting

Phone shrills crack my morning
like too-dry leather.

Its voice blares,
the rude houseguest

who won't help herself,
calling out for me to bring this or that.

Each time it shakes to life
I quicken my step, suspend my breath,

but never the voice I desire.
Day after day, disappointment

settles like dust, until finally
the ringing becomes mundane,

my breathing, easy.
I barely notice the change.

And then the call
containing your voice.

Right on cue, I falter.

The Fall

Through static
on the line
come words
of repentance
but there is no
confessor here.

And yet,
hope rises from me
thick as smoke
from a thurible,
perfumed,
heady,
intoxicating.

Doubts

Downtown dressing room
regards me.

Mirror eyes pass no judgment
but reveal misgiving.

Pale rose lingerie,
filigree against skin.

I tell myself I'll give
unlimited affection

to welcome you home, but
how many of your heart's chambers

still swell with love for me?
It is a question worth asking.

The delicacy of lace
is fragile,

no match for the weight
of our reunion.

Force

This afternoon sky whispers rain.
Blue gray and yellow white
touch without blending.
Naked trees spiderweb across the horizon;
birds catch in their net.

You returned for seventeen days
saying you could not explain
why you left, but your words
were as empty
as your eyes and heart.
No peace
for either of us;
you had other fires burning,
impossible to extinguish.

The moment of your second leaving
dissolves into another time
when a bride kissed a groom
and the world
was bright and wide.
Voices long silent
sound again,
faces blurred by time
come softly into focus.

This afternoon sky whispers rain;
there can be no holding it back,
the force of nature as strong
as a tornado
claiming its path.
It will have its way.

Division

Come see for yourself,
you say. *Anna would be pleased.*

My heart stumbles over its rhythm,
loses count of its beat.
How easily her name
rolls from your tongue,
a landslide tumbling
toward my home's thin walls.

It is your garden you wish me to see.

In the aftermath of our failure,
I accept your departure.
As if you were a ship
sailing its first voyage,
I blessed your start
with daffodil bulbs
split from beds of my own,
once ours,
but now pushing their roots
into other soil.

Next spring
they will lift frilled faces
toward the light.
They are discreet
and will not speak
of their time with me.

At the end

of this thorny path,
a divorce waits;
from a distance, it watches,
chews its fingernails
and curses my slow step.

I will not join it, not yet.

I do not drag time
as punishment for you.
Instead it's one last thing
I can hold; this life we built
is a broken thing
but pieces still catch
fragments of sunlight.

If my heart lingers
in its playhouse,
forgive it;
it is merely being theatrical,
prolonging a scene to
avoid our curtain's fall,
postpone the final bow.

It convinces not even itself
these days.

Uprooted

Listen, girl: I can explain things now. Before, I was just an embryo locked in the tissues of your heart, mouth taped shut by your youth, that turncoat.

Look at these photos you kept, age-curled but proof of ecstasy, before vows were spoken and imaginary boundaries staked, and you, with that smile, looking like you'd plucked the biggest prize in God's goodie bag. The two of you, side by side, no margin between your skin and his. See how he towers above you? You liked that. So masculine. But here's what you forgot: Eros, sly boy, sometimes delivers dreadful joy.

Flip through faded letters, your mother saved them, yours again now. Stand under the waterfall of words you loosed on her. Float as she did on syllables you sent, how idyllic.

You kept secret the deceit he tracked in, but it wrapped itself around you like bittersweet on a maple, twisting and encircling until its weight toppled you. Uprooted and in your own home. The humiliation when neighbors saw your leaves on the ground and broken roots dangling mid-air.

No denying any longer, your boy's a rotter.

A convert, you'll try to preach, but girls won't believe. Blinded with youth, power untapped, they deliver themselves to love like a suicide to oncoming train.

Inaccessible

Warrior

I melt into the south of France;
the heat of Arles licks my face,
presses against my eyes,
steals moisture wherever it can,
leaves me shriveled, hollow.

My breath is shallow and short.
Like the old women wandering the streets
collecting bits and pieces
for an evening meal,
I walk only on the shaded sides
of narrow lanes, moving slowly,
as if I had a hundred years
before morning breaks time
into past and present.

I belong in the ruined passages
of Les Baux de Provence.
Along the mountain's spine
among the scattered bones of a castle
bleached white by the sun's
persistent stare,
I recognize myself.

Stone steps, concave from wear
over hundreds of years,
lead only to a broken wall, a useless arch.
Wildflowers and grass lounge on every surface;
they have no need for caution;
feet no longer trudge here.
A solitary wall holds a memory of tapestries,
the force of life that once pushed and pulled,
while the outline of a window
peers across the valley floor.

Autumn days urge patience,
promise a coming touch
from spring's soft hand.

Moment of Stillness

In Paris, I sit in a Metro
car on the lavender
line, its semicircular route
stretching luxuriously
up from Balard
and down to Pointe du Lac,
a cat draped on a chair's back.

Last week, there was
a three-hour delay;
riders settled in for the wait.

A man had dropped himself
neatly onto the tracks,
submitting to the oncoming train
like a despairing lover,
a weary supplicant.
His life's ending
arrived on a schedule of his creation,
not an unknown TBA date.

Endings require time
for sorting and cleaning.
Everyone knows this
except those
who depart first.

Lullaby

She has moved from one country
to another.
I say she is brave, but
she says when one has no home
the country does not matter.

As she weaves this sentence
unshed tears sparkle.

I nod.
The rootless
recognize each other;
we remember home
but see it is lost.
The past cradles
our memories,
hums a lullaby,
a promise of hurts
that will subside.

Unmoored

A simple cell within the Conciergerie,
final dwelling place of Marie Antoinette.
Outside glass panes, bars
curve like fangs,
weapons of a large beast
bent on destruction.

The interior courtyard
where imprisoned females
could do laundry, walk in the sun,
sit for a short chat
is small, surrounded
by walls and windows,
a hundred places
to hold those who watched.

For a moment
I am alone in their hard garden;
At the stone table, I wonder
if her fingers played
across the rough surface
as mine do now.

I consider the height
from which she fell
and think it not so rare
to go from young, unwise queen,
sheltered and protected,
to despised and doomed,
another female unmoored,
unwanted.

Without

Where the Seine hugs the curve
of Ile Saint-Louis,
a solitary swan glides, then
rests; ducks tolerate
the newcomer.

Day after day it floats
alone on gray water.
Perhaps the City of Light
offers tonic to a partner's fate,
and relief,
long-lasting or not, is
welcome.

Among makeshift circle of friends,
the swan keeps its counsel,
preening at the close
of another winter's day.

Surrender

I arrive in Bruges
on a smothering bus
wishing I'd taken the train
but not regretting the beauty
of Belgium countryside
seen leisurely.

I wander serpentine streets,
cross foot bridges too narrow
to walk beside someone.

In the town's center, a church
boasts a drop of Christ's blood.
Pilgrims travel far to see it;
crossing the threshold,
they weep like long absent
children come home
to family's welcoming arms.

In religious realms, a relic
is treasured, never
discarded, never
left behind.

Of being beloved,
I must not be covetous.

Ebb

Bruges, Belgium, enjoyed an important role in history because of sea trade until the Zwijn estuary silted up in the fifteenth century.

How did Bruges adapt?
Once, her face was cupped,
held gently by the sea.
She knew her place,
felt safe and flourished.
Ships came to call;
she welcomed them like neighbors
bearing baskets of bounty,
stopping by for a good gossip.

But the sea grew distracted.
Domesticity chafed.
Bruges lost her figure,
her skin sallow, wrinkled.
Too often, the sea spoke in tones
no longer dulcet,
left silt lying around like
day-old socks.
Ships, once plentiful,
stopped calling.

Still, Bruges was unprepared
when the sea's gaze wandered
westward where the sun reclined,
sultry and inviting.
Wildness rocked its soul.
The sea had no recourse;
it must follow or die.

Bruges stayed in her home,
gazed through salt-soiled windows,
knew she'd never again witness
soft moonlight dance
on cresting waves.

Easements

Aphrodite

Like the son of Belus,
I carved an image of you,
entreated love, counted
as pleasure each agony
as I waited.

I can admit it now;
your arrival was my doing,
my undoing.

At the start, we were star dwellers,
the rhythm of life, steady.
But secret slices of evenings
saw you conjuring. Bliss-blind,
I neither saw nor heard, slumbered
as sage blades of grass
whispered tales of your prowl,
your hunt for another.

Our eight-year reign at an end,
does Aphrodite regret our reversal?
If so, she does not speak of it to me.
She frolics, net-wrapped limbs
enticing new eyes,
conquering as she pleases,
assured renewal awaits her
in the sea.

I will duck my head, feel
the sting of salt,
surface
clean and new.

Transformation

Thunder rumbles
and I feel walls shake.

Unease ripples;
childish fears stir.

Somewhere rivers are rising,
churning whitecaps, dislodging logs.

Lifting themselves over banks,
waters congregate,

loiter in fields,
leave behind a trail

of mud and debris like
teenagers on spring break.

I contemplate changes;
the world reshapes itself with every storm.

Outside, above the rain,
a songbird trills its indifference.

Reach

A person with brain trauma
must relearn things,
forgetfulness, forgiven.
A part of the brain is dead;
tissues no longer transmit messages.
The body adapts.

When the heart
receives the blow,
discolored affection
does not show
on scans; the bearer
is expected to regain
full function, move
forward. Weary
friends warn
against bitterness.

Alone, I weed near a poplar stump,
its surface gray, no hope of life.
Oblivious, its edges are fertile.
Green sprouts lift clumsy leaves,
anxious to start again.

Endings beget beginnings;
the shape of new life is different
but it breathes
and reaches for the sun
just the same.

The Nature of Things

Our lives, spirals,
grooves in soft earth
like those behind a plow
in freshly-turned field,

each path unique but similar,
a labyrinth we all follow.
Our mothers, the starting point.
Our loves and losses become
details etched in stones
lining our walk,
leading to the stopping point
where a final breath holds itself
at journey's end.

Perhaps we are like water
hurtling toward, then over the falls.
That we are allowed even once
to crash into pools,
curl ourselves around rocks,
and overflow banks
is enough.

Sunset Blessing

Bed rails frame him as he sleeps,
small trellises securing a sapling.

His chest rises and falls, delicate,
like the gray titmouse who visits our feeder.

I am shelter,
building around him a protective nest.

At the right moment
I will withstand his flight.

Let him soar and rise
on swelling updrafts.

Although you will not watch
the slip of his hours into years,

perhaps you will bear witness
from your own distant mountaintop.

Epilogue: Surfaces, ii

Here is the dream again,
the field, the moonlight.
But this time
I am the chimney;
inside my granite coat
my arms hang limply,
this time, no lichens on my eyes.
I see you stacking kindling
in my fireplace;
you do not see me.
You strike a match
but I allow a draft of wind
to blow softly down my throat,
extinguish your flame.
Time after time you try to burn,
to blacken me with soot;
each time I defeat you.
I bear you no ill will.
I have ceased suffering
the singe of your desires.
I am granite.
I will not crumble.

About the Author

Peggy Goodwin Hammond grew up in Apex, North Carolina, when it was a small town surrounded by farms. She earned her MA in English Literature from North Carolina State University and taught a variety of college English courses for many years. Her poetry has been nominated for Best of the Net, and it appears in several national and international publications, including *Rogue Agent, Two Thirds North, Cordella, The Comstock Review, Waterwheel Review, Jabberwock Review, Adelaide Literary Magazine, Pangyrus, West Trade Review, Fragmented Voices, Dodging The Rain,* and others. Her full-length play *A Little Bit of Destiny* was produced by OdysseyStage Theatre in Durham, North Carolina. Learn more at www.peggyhammondpoetry.com.

www.ingramcontent.com/pod-product-compliance
Lightning Source LLC
Chambersburg PA
CBHW031205160426
43193CB00008B/509